For Satori

哲理

First published 2015
Published by Butterfly Books Limited

A CIP catalogue record for this book is available from the British Library.

ISBN: 978-0-9932769-0-3

Printed in England.

A special thanks to Corey Brotherson (Editor)

www.butterflybooks.uk

SECOND PRINTING – MARCH 2016

My Mummy is an ENGINEER

By Kerrine Bryan & Jason Bryan

Illustrated by Marissa Peguinho

My mummy is an engineer,
working hard throughout the year.

She always has an early start,
and wears a dress that looks very smart.

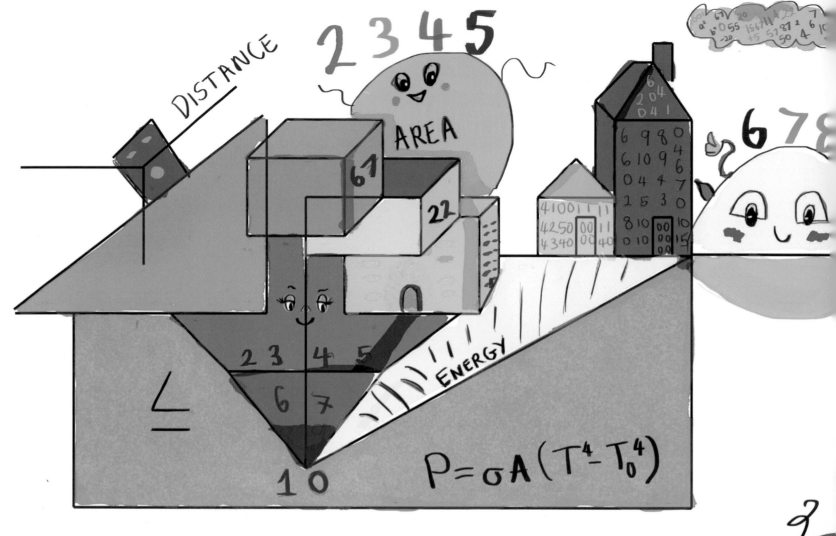

My mummy's job sounds like fun,
solving puzzles one by one.
Engineering uses science and maths,
to answer questions during tricky tasks.

$4 + 5 = \dots$

$9 - 2 = \dots$

$10 \div 2 = \dots$

$3 \times 4 = \dots$

In the morning meeting mummy makes tough decisions,
to ensure we have power for our televisions.

She sits at her desk in the afternoon,
designing space rockets that fly to the moon.

My mummy's job sounds like fun,
solving puzzles one by one.
Engineering is working in teams,
creating real things that once were dreams.

Sometimes mummy works on-site,
wearing a vest that's **very** bright.
There are tractors and cranes and machines that GRIND.
Construction teams build what mummy has designed.

My mummy's job sounds like fun,
solving puzzles one by one.

Engineering has many extremes,
from hot-air balloons to submarines.

There are so many things mummy has engineered,
about them all you have to hear:

She's designed the **TALLEST** buildings ever,
and beautiful bridges - she is **oh**-so clever!

Railways with trains that go super fast,
and racing cars that go zOOming past!

Paralympians' special limbs,
my mummy has designed such incredible things.

My mummy's job sounds like fun,
but there's another task when the work is done.

When she comes home and I've had my tea,
she reads a bedtime story to me!